BLESSINGS TO INSPIRE

BLESSINGS TO INSPIRE

Devotions, Empowerment Points, Prayers,
and Affirmations for the Spirit and Soul

JACQUELINE D. STINSON

FOREWORD BY
KELLEY STEPHENSON-WHITE

Xulon Press
2301 Lucien Way #415
Maitland, FL 32751
407.339.4217
www.xulonpress.com

Blessings To Inspire
by Jacqueline D. Stinson
Foreword by Kelley Stephenson-White

Printed in the United States of America.

ISBN-13: 9781545619346

Dedication

"And we know that in all things God works for the good of those who love him, who have been called according to his purpose." *(Romans 8:28 NIV)*

This book is dedicated to the late Freddie Lee and Estella Stinson. All things have a purpose and season in the eyes of the Lord regardless of how man views them. I'm forever grateful that He chose you both to conceive and bring forth a life overflowing with words to bless heaven and earth. Missing and loving you always!

Acknowledgments

To my Lord and Savior Jesus Christ, who makes all things possible. You could have chosen many, but You gave me my own unique voice, primarily through written words, and saw fit to use it for Your glory. I'm humbled and forever grateful. I could never love You as much as You love me, but I sincerely love You with all my heart.

To Anthony Lee McCannon, my son and only child. You know I would give my life for yours. You're such a blessing to me, and you have inspired this book in many ways. I thank the Lord for the wonderful man you've become. You have much to give. Keep trusting in the Lord and moving toward your dreams and destiny. Loving you always.

To Kelley Stephenson-White, my little sister-cousin. What a powerful blessing and inspiration you are in my life. You're an awesome and true woman of God. Over thirty years spent apart was absolutely too long, but we both know that the Lord doesn't make mistakes. His divine plan and timing is always perfect. One thing is certain, I know you're always in my corner, being true and desperately praying for me and our entire family. Early in the mornings on many occasions, we've met the Lord together at the throne of grace. The Word of the Lord clearly states, "For where two or three gather in my name, there am I with them" (Matthew 18:20 NIV). I'm grateful for your unselfish support. You petitioned and obeyed the voice of God to go before me and introduce this book to the world. Love you forever.

To Mary E. Webb and Shirnette Allison (my aunts); and to Frances Stephenson-Ross, Betty Richardson, and Linda Owens (my cousins). Living on this side without my parents hasn't been easy, but I'm grateful to the Lord for those full of life watching over and encouraging me in many and peculiar ways. Although there are others, I chose to honor you, a few of my elders. Thankful for your inspiration behind this book. Even the mishaps and misunderstandings in our family have revealed awesome revelations and purpose for growth. Thank you for praying with and for me, particularly my dear cousins Frances and Betty who sacrifice early Saturday mornings to meet me in prayer for ourselves, our entire family, and many others. Loving you always.

To my remaining family members, bless you for your prayers and words of encouragement. Let's continue to stand in faith; there is still plenty of work to be done in all of us. Love you much.

To Yvette Davis, my sister in Christ and friend. Thank you from the bottom of my heart for your willingness to support this book. You truly took the time to share from a heart of love. Blessings and love always.

To Corlos Morris, my brother in Christ, neighbor for nearly a decade, and friend. I'm grateful for your divine brotherly love. Thank you for being a prayer and accountability partner, and for all of your support. All that you've given toward this book is greatly appreciated. Love you forever.

To my Christian Pen Pal friends, I'm continuously thanking the Lord and praying He will keep watch over each and every one of you. You've truly been a blessing and inspiration by your sharing and praying through numerous correspondences. Continue to trust Him and build on everything the Lord has placed inside you. Peace, love, and blessings always.

To my spiritual leaders and to the remaining brothers and sisters in the kingdom, thank you for pouring the Word of God into my spirit, for your many prayers, and for your words of encouragement. Blessings and love always.

Contents

Foreword

$\mathcal{J}$acqueline and I were reunited in the latter part of 2015 after over three decades without contact. Although our fond memories of one another are primarily from our early childhood years, the love we possess never ceased. We refer to one another as "sister-cousin." In the midst of our reconnection, we instantly felt an anointing and spiritual bond resembling that of true sisters in the kingdom, although in the flesh we are cousins in kinship.

This woman of God is anointed and gifted, and she encompasses an abundance of love for our Father God, His people, and the biblical Word. Her willingness to minister and encourage others far surpasses anyone I've ever encountered in my almost forty years of life. She is genuine in her walk with the Lord, and she constantly researches ways to effectively spread the gospel of Jesus Christ.

You'll find this book to be helpful in your journey to enhance your understanding of what the Lord can and will do in any circumstance for you as an individual and for your family. The brief yet informative devotions, empowerment points, prayers, and affirmations will encourage and help guide you on your spiritual walk. You'll find yourself emotionally and spiritually connected to the messages while being driven by the Word of God. There were quite a few that resonated with me, but "A Rider or Helper and Provider" stuck out in particular. It speaks to the troubled and confused person battling relationship issues, whether they are single or married. This entry provides a clear and concise description of the roles of a man and woman along with clarifying the Lord's expectations in this area according to His holy Word.

The devotions and Scriptures annotated in this book have encouraged me to continue seeking God first in all I do and contend with. Although at times I feel as if I am alone, I'm reminded by thought, action, Scripture, or devotion that God is always with me. I have found this book to be spiritually uplifting and motivating. I pray that it will have the same impact on you and many more.

Kelley Stephenson-White

Introduction

"Being confident of this, that he who began a good work in you will carry it on to completion until the day of Christ Jesus." *(Philippians 1:6 NIV)*

Whether they are written or spoken, words are powerful. Numerous devotions produced by several different inspirational authors have had a profound impact on my life, particularly during the most difficult seasons. Their words encouraged the gift our Father has given me to share with the world.

This book has been started, put down, and picked back up more than one could ever imagine. Some would probably say this is due to much procrastination and laziness. Although I'm in agreement to some extent, I sincerely believe that there is a divine plan that includes the appointed timing and seasons for all things to manifest. The father of all lies indeed premeditated schemes and attempted assassination against this vision to prevent many from being *blessed and inspired.* As you can see, the liar, killer, and thief didn't prevail.

Many of the devotions in this book were inspired by real-life experiences, and some entries were recorded in my personal journals. Some were written when the sun shone the brightest, others were written in mighty dark places, and several more come from areas of my soul that bear the sign "Work in Progress." Yes, it's been written for me too. Whatever emanates in this lifetime, we all need true words of encouragement from different voices along the way.

The sole purpose of this book is to exhort your spirit (the inner part of man that directly connects with our Lord and understands spiritual things) and soul (the mind, will, and emotions of man).

Some experiences that affect our spirit and soul are pleasant, and others are filled with rivalry. There is evidence and testaments of both here. Every situation and detail in our life has the ability to generate something prominent within and beyond ourselves.

This devotional invites you into experiences, testimonies, and a quiet place with the Lord at any pace and time. The key Scriptures will lead you to dive deeper into His Word, and empowerment points will help you ponder and apply the teachings to your life. The short prayers are primarily written in the voice of the first person. I encourage you to make them personal and to utilize them as a model to create your own prayer journal as you release, talk to the Lord, and allow Him to speak to you. Then, affirm the truth over your life and circumstances.

As you meditate on the subsequent contents, my deepest prayer is that you'll feel the hand and existence of the Lord. He is always there, blessing and empowering you to be who you were created to be. Our Lord is the King of all, and He will complete what He has started right on time. If you don't know Him, I have great anticipation that you'll leave these pages with a burning desire to draw closer to the Lord. There is nothing in this lifetime that you will encounter and endure alone. He loves you beyond measure, and He had you on His mind long before this book was embedded in the womb of this chosen vessel. Without a shadow of a doubt, you are certainly *blessed* and worthy to be *inspired*.

Blessings for Any Day

A Heart of Gratitude

> "In everything give thanks; for this is the will of God
> in Christ Jesus for you."
>
> *(1 Thessalonians 5:18 NKJV)*

One morning, my son shared that he had been involved in a vehicle accident the night before. After learning of a young woman's demise as the result of another car accident later that day, I was even more grateful that my son's accident wasn't more serious.

Anyone who has experienced a much different and more unfortunate outcome may ask, "How can I be thankful when I'm grieved?" The word everything in this passage of Scripture is the key. Our God understands and comforts when we've been afflicted with pain, grief, and disappointments, and He also joins us in celebrating our victories.

We never know what will stand before us on any given day. Surely all of us can reflect back over our lives with appreciative hearts and see the perfect will of God in every situation. It may be difficult to imagine and feel at the time, but even the most painful and devastating experiences work together for something good and are worth giving thanks for.

If you haven't already, give Him your whole heart right now. Let it overflow with thanksgiving, even amid the tears, regardless of what time it is in your life.

Empowerment Point: Appreciate the good and bad seasons because you never know what may arise from them.

Prayer: Dear Heavenly Father, today I thank You for everything in my life. When it's difficult to understand what's going on, remind me to trust You. All I've endured was purposed to build my inner strength. In Jesus' name I pray, amen.

Affirmation: Not just for some things, but in all things I will be grateful.

A Lifeline for a Lifetime

"He reached down from on high and took hold of me;
he drew me out of deep waters." *(Psalm 18:16 NIV)*

Our deep waters could be unforeseen circumstances beyond our control or the adversary taking his best shot at us. Then again, we may discover ourselves in way over our heads because of our disobedience or because we have chosen to lean on our own intellect.

The psalmist knew in his times of trouble exactly who to depend on for his rescue. He didn't turn to family and friends, but called out to the Lord and He did answer. Throughout David's entire life and walk with the Lord, He was always there.

Are you in too deep? The Lord is standing by, waiting to throw you the rope. It's accessible to you with not only hope but eternal security. The Lord will surely swim the deepest waters to free you.

Empowerment Point: People you depend on may leave you hanging, but you can rely on the Lord anytime.

Prayer: Dear Heavenly Father, You are faithful and compassionate. When I've traveled way outside of the safety zone in life, You're always willing and waiting to liberate me. You heard my weeping under the currents, and You acted out of nothing but love. In Jesus' name I pray, amen.

Affirmation: My life is in the hands of the very best.

A Rider or Helper and Provider

"And the LORD God said, 'It is not good that man should be alone; I will make him a helper comparable to him.'" *(Genesis 2:18 NKJV)*

"But if anyone does not provide for his own, and especially for those of his household, he has denied the faith and is worse than an unbeliever."
(1 Timothy 5:8 NKJV)

The Lord created woman to be by a man's side as his wife and helpmate. It's a husband's duty to protect and provide for his wife and family. The covenant between the two should include the Lord, and be a ministry that reverences Him.

Many live how they choose, dishonoring the Lord. People come into others' lives with schemes to rob, take advantage, and destroy, not realizing that they are being used by the adversary.

Inquire of yourself: Is she truly a good candidate for the "help wanted" ad, or is she just a Barbie doll? Has he proven during courtship that he would cover you, meet your needs, and give his life if it came down to it? Seek the Lord, and believe that He has the right person just for you.

Empowerment Point: Don't permit your loneliness to lead you to make poor choices.

Prayer: Dear Heavenly Father, it's Your desire for joy and peace to flow in my relationships with others. Whether I'm in a season of singleness or married, help me to live by Your Word. Reveal to me when my connections are not moving me closer to You. In Jesus' name I pray, amen.

Affirmation: I am worth waiting for.

A True Friend

"One who has unreliable friends soon comes to ruin,
but there is a friend who sticks closer than a brother."
(Proverbs 18:24 NIV)

*D*uring our early childhood years, most of us claimed many friends. If they treated us nicely and shared their goodies, they instantly became our friend.

King Solomon shares great wisdom regarding friendships. Our Father desires for us to be in relationships with others, and He has done mighty works through numerous connections. We should keep in mind that He wants us to be wise in selecting friends.

Disappointments often come from relationships. Even in facing being let down by others, we have assurance through God's Word and our own personal testaments of His faithfulness that He is the best friend we could ever have.

Don't rest in discouragement when those in your life don't behave as you expect. Turn to the One who is always there for you, who is available at all times, and who has promised to be a legitimate friend until the end.

Empowerment Point: Expect and accept nothing but the best out of relationships.

Prayer: Dear Heavenly Father, I'm so glad You are a friend of mine. Lead me and open doors to healthy and honorable relationships. Give me a mindset and an ear to hear Your voice when I've opened the door to the wrong people. In Jesus' name I pray, amen.

Affirmation: I have a friend who will be with me now and even into eternity.

All Things in Time

"He has made everything beautiful in its time. Also He has put eternity in their hearts, except that no one can find out the work that God does from beginning to end." *(Ecclesiastes 3:11 NKJV)*

We are all in a waiting room for something. Some are anticipating answered prayers for family. Others await a promotion on the job. The list of hopes, dreams, and expectations is extensive. Patience and trust is essential for all who wait. We focus greatly on our earthly time, but God sees all things from an eternal standpoint. We can't begin to fathom what and how He is working out of sight for us.

A deceased but very well-known entertainer once stated in an interview, "All things in time. We want our lives to be like McDonald's. We want things and things to happen right now." In so many words, the artist continued to express how it just doesn't work that way.

Whatever it is you've been waiting on, and regardless of how long you've been waiting, trust the splendor of God's timing.

Empowerment Point: Be patient with yourself and others, and most importantly, know that God is always right on schedule.

Prayer: Dear Heavenly Father, You know what's best for me and when to release it. In this world, anxiousness is always an option, and it's difficult to escape. Right now, I turn it all over to You and put my hope in Your perfect timing. In Jesus' name I pray, amen.

Affirmation: I will wait on God.

Because You Showed Me How

"Follow my example, as I follow the example of
Christ." *(1 Corinthians 11:1 NIV)*

*B*eing a parent is an awesome experience and a blessing.
Of course, along with the good, there are challenges and
uncertainties in this role. Often, these famous parenting questions
are asked: "Why did you do that?" and "Why did you say that?" In
some instances, during a reprimand, many parents may be challenged
to step back and examine their own behavior to see what action the
child was observing versus the words being said.

The apostle Paul expressed to the Corinthian church that he
wasn't just a teacher and preacher, but that he led a life that was
pleasing to Christ. Jesus lived a life and demonstrated all throughout
the Bible how we should model Him. His example wasn't just for
our own well-being, but also for us to represent in a godly way for
our offspring and others.

Live your life based on demonstration, particularly in front of
your children. It's the only way some will ever come face-to-face
with Christ and see the truth.

Empowerment Point: Others are paying attention to your walk.

Prayer: Dear Heavenly Father, Your allowing the glory of Christ to
shine through me is a wonderful gift. When I'm in the presence of
my children and others, let them see You. In all my ways, strengthen
me to follow and be more like You. In Jesus' name I pray, amen.

Affirmation: My presentation matters to God.

Blessed by a Stranger

"I am sending him to you for this very purpose, that
he may know your circumstances and comfort your
hearts." *(Colossians 4:8 NKJV)*

One day, a winter hat embellished with beautiful colors on a
street vendor's table caught my attention. A conversation
ensued between me and the vendor about the goodness of the Lord.
There was such a divine connection and expression of encouragement
in our conversation.

When the Lord wakes us up each morning and start us on our way,
we never know who will be placed in our path. My encounter could
have turned out differently on this particular day. The vendor could
have received my money and told me to have a nice day. Instead, a
blessing was released by this individual that lingered for quite some
time just because a stranger unselfishly took the time to talk.

Be alert and willing to exhort others, whether they are familiar
or unfamiliar. You have the power and authority to do so.

Empowerment Point: You are blessed when you bless someone else.

Prayer: Dear Heavenly Father, angels are all around me. Your
greatness is revealed when we encourage and are encouraged by
others. I am blessed to be a blessing. In Jesus' name I pray, amen.

Affirmation: I will pass on the same hope the Lord gives to me.

Called to Suffer

> "We are hard pressed on every side, but not crushed;
> perplexed, but not in despair; persecuted, but not
> abandoned; struck down, but not destroyed."
> *(2 Corinthians 4:8–9 NIV)*

*S*uffering is something our flesh doesn't like to endure. However, we are exhorted in God's Word that afflictions are all worthwhile, and that they have no power to take us down for the count.

We all have purpose in the kingdom, and we will all experience unwelcome difficulty. In the midst of our difficulties and persecution, we have to accept that if we want to inherit what's on the other side of opposition, all that the Lord has for us, we must go through suffering just as the Son did.

Stand firm and know that your enemies can't do you any harm. A circumstance only lasts for a while, and there is certainly a blessing to claim when you're enduring it for the glory of Christ.

Empowerment Point: Think it not strange, and go on through the process.

Prayer: Dear Heavenly Father, I will never know the true depth of the agony Christ Jesus bore. When it's my time and You're molding and shaping, help me not to fight. It was good that affliction came upon me, and there is nothing too hard to handle with You. In Jesus' name I pray, amen.

Affirmation: God is with me in times of suffering.

Catch Me if You Will

"Therefore let us not judge one another anymore, but rather resolve this, not to put a stumbling block or a cause to fall in our brother's way."

(Romans 14:13 NKJV)

The adversary will use any available body, but it's even more disheartening when brothers and sisters in the kingdom of God are willing to see one another fall. As Paul conveyed to the Romans, we all belong to God, whether we're weak or strong.

How can you catch another who may be weak and headed into danger? Physical action isn't always required; you can also pray that their spiritual eyes and entire being will be opened to the revelation of God. If you are so led by the Holy Spirit, share a testimony about what God has revealed and done in your life. Love them enough to be bold in an appropriate manner to say, "Get yourself together because your soul means just that much to me." Let them know from your heart that you'll hold their hand and walk with them through their trial.

Empowerment Point: Help another soar to their greatest potential versus allowing them to sink.

Prayer: Dear Heavenly Father, regardless of what's happening, help me to view others the way You see them. Let my walk empower another to rise above their trials. Position my heart to be available for intercession on others' behalf. In Jesus' name I pray, amen.

Affirmation: I can play a positive role in my brothers' and sisters' success.

Celebrate You

"This is the day the LORD has made;
We will rejoice and be glad in it." *(Psalm 118:24 NIV)*

For a variety of reasons, many people feel that they can't celebrate themselves. Some look for others to congratulate and recognize them, and they're still waiting for that recognition. Celebration doesn't have to involve a special occasion or require splurging money. In the Lord's eyes, every day is worth celebrating not only Him but yourself.

If you want to plan a celebration, plan it! You don't have to mimic the Joneses and purchase the finest china and brand-name products. If you can afford to break the bank at the checkout, then break it! Recognize that it's the Lord's day in which He has created, and He permitted you to breathe and rejoice in it.

Empowerment Point: You get only one life to live; revel in it.

Prayer: Dear Heavenly Father, You're my primary reason to celebrate each new day. You gave me life and seasons to celebrate in it to the utmost. Whether it's a unique occasion or not, I'm looking forward to the days ahead and all You have in store. In Jesus' name I pray, amen.

Affirmation: I will rejoice at all times not just because of who Christ is, but for the life He has given me.

Clean Up

"Thus says the Lord God: 'On the day that I cleanse
you from all your iniquities, I will also enable you
to dwell in the cities, and the ruins shall be rebuilt.'"
(Ezekiel 36:33 NKJV)

The Lord spoke through a sermon from the pulpit, "Clean your
house up. When your surroundings change, you will change
and see things differently." The words moved me in a profound
way. Shortly afterward while I was cleaning, I moved a chair in the
process, and there lay a precious sterling silver bracelet given to me
as a Christmas gift.

The Lord reveals Himself in some kind of way in every detail of
our lives. The discovery of this gift reminded me about the people
of Israel who were living as they chose in disobedience to the Lord,
not honoring Him in the land. The Lord's desire was to clean them
up, taking away the filth of their flesh, and He promised that He
would do it.

It's important that you allow the Lord to purify your spiritual
temples through confession and repentance. This makes way for you
to see Him in a different light, to come back into His presence, and
to receive restoration, which permits blessings to flow freely.

Empowerment Point: No matter what in you is messy, it's never
too late to come for purification.

Prayer: Dear Heavenly Father, it's awesome to know that I don't
have to stay in contamination. The cleansing won't happen overnight,
but right now I open my heart and give You access to the inner
man. Because of Your great work progressing in me every day, I can
reclaim what's been lost and begin again. In Jesus' name I pray, amen.

Affirmation: My Lord will cleanse and reestablish me in Him.

Don't Worry, You're Far More Important

> "Look at the birds of the air; they do not sow or reap or store away in barns, and yet your heavenly Father feeds them. Are you not much more valuable than they? Can any one of you by worrying add a single hour to your life?" *(Matthew 6:26–27 NIV)*

We live in an era of constant change. The cost of living for a family to survive and make provision for basic essentials can be overwhelming. In this passage, Jesus teaches and reminds us that we are children of God and that He cares about our needs. He expresses just how much we mean to Him.

Jesus asks us to examine how the birds survive, but most importantly to realize that if God cares that much about the animals, then He is even more concerned about us human beings. You may have many needs, and you could be feeling as if your prayers have not been heard. Instead of harboring anxiety, imagine God standing before you with His hands stretched toward you, releasing everything you need. Worry does more harm than good, and God's Word makes it clear that it buys no additional time on this earth.

Understand that God hasn't forgotten about you and that there is no reason to be anxious about anything. Before He formed the earth and created the first man, He knew exactly what you needed. Therefore, strive not to spend time fretting about your necessities, but trust the One who cares about you the most.

Empowerment Point: He never fails; He will come through.

Prayer: Dear Heavenly Father, thank You for letting me know that my life and needs matter. I know that no matter what I need in this life, You're able. I believe that You alone will not only supply my needs but those of my entire family as well. In Jesus' name I pray, amen.

Affirmation: My Father cares for me beyond what I could ever imagine.

Fight with Love

"Love suffers long and is kind; love does not envy; love does not parade itself, is not puffed up; does not behave rudely, does not seek its own, is not provoked, thinks no evil; does not rejoice in iniquity, but rejoices in the truth; bears all things, believes all things, hopes all things, endures all things."

(1 Corinthians 13:4–7 NKJV)

One morning, a devotion spoke to me regarding an unsettling message I had received from a childhood friend. Although this person continued to be negative, my response reflected love. Sometimes sincere love requires you to apologize and ask for forgiveness even when you've done nothing wrong. It ushers the presence of God and His divine love into your midst.

Whatever your issue may be or with whom, choose to respond with love versus spending time and energy on damaging emotions. You never know how God may use the situation for your good. He is love at all times, and He expects us to exemplify the same toward others even when it's difficult.

Empowerment Point: Sometimes being the bigger person requires giving up the desire to be the winner.

Prayer: Dear Heavenly Father, there is no greater love than Yours. It conquers and surpasses all things. Just because of that, I'm thankful that all of my battles were already won long before they began. In Jesus' name I pray, amen.

Affirmation: I know the love of God will always prevail.

Follow the Leader

"'Come, follow me,' Jesus said, 'and I will send you out to fish for people.' At once they left their nets and followed him." *(Mark 1:17–18 NIV)*

When Jesus called His first disciples, they gave no hesitation or back talk. They immediately responded to His leading. We can only imagine what they would have missed out on had they not obeyed. When we allow the Savior to lead our lives, others will see Him as we encourage them to surrender their lives and pursue Him.

Is He the center of your life? Perhaps you've veered off course and followed the wrong voice. Pray and ask Christ to guide you back on the right path with Him. Christ is faithfully and patiently waiting on you.

Empowerment Point: He knows the right road even when it doesn't make sense.

Prayer: Dear Heavenly Father, You will never lead me wrong. Teach me how to listen to and obey Your voice. At times when I deviate in the opposite direction, thank You for loving me enough to do whatever it takes to draw me back to You. In Jesus' name I pray, amen.

Affirmation: He is my keeper and director.

From Sorrow to Rejoicing

"And God will wipe away every tear from their eyes;
there shall be no more death, nor sorrow, nor crying.
There shall be no more pain, for the former things
have passed away." *(Revelation 21:4 NKJV)*

A cousin and I had just returned from the mortuary. As we entered my mother's apartment, somehow my cousin accidentally set off pepper spray inside her purse. All we could do for several minutes was cough and gasp, and suddenly we burst out laughing. We recalled my mother's well-known sense of humor, and it was as if she was right there, laughing, urging us to carry on with life, and letting us know that there was no sadness in her new life.

The Word of God tells us that the New Jerusalem where our Father dwells is perfect. There is no grief as in this troubled world.

It's not easy, but with God by your side, it is indeed possible to rejoice when loved ones transition. I don't wish that you have a surprise encounter like mine, but you must live on. It's alright to laugh through the tears, even if it's just for a moment.

Empowerment Point: When it feels like you won't rejoice again, believe that you will.

Prayer: Dear Heavenly Father, You are a comforter in my times of sorrow. Your holy Word assures me that I never have to walk down the road alone. You are the center of my joy no matter what may come. In Jesus' name I pray, amen.

Affirmation: There will be times of mourning, but the joy of the Lord is my strength.

Go Beyond Yourself

"For even the Son of Man came not to be served but to serve others and to give his life as a ransom for many." *(Mark 10:45 NIV)*

Christ came with a significant purpose and paid a high price. By no means did He have room for selfishness in His heart. He demonstrates to us that it requires a humble spirit to lay one's desires aside to serve another.

Many aspire to receive the highest of honors, but never consider the needs of others. It doesn't always require money or material possessions to serve. We pass our fellow man all throughout the day, and we can meet needs in a variety of ways. Our communities are suffering while many focus on serving and giving on the inside of the church's walls and never on the outside.

As you cross off tasks on your "things to do list," think of someone else today and how you may share the Savior's love and blessings with them. Give Christ praise for providing you the opportunity to help serve another.

Empowerment Point: It's rewarding to serve others.

Prayer: Dear Heavenly Father, it's never all about me. Whenever there is another in need, help me to be sensitive to the leading of the Spirit. You've exemplified for all humanity a true servant's attitude. In Jesus' name I pray, amen.

Affirmation: Because of Christ and His unselfish service for me, I'm empowered to meet the needs of others.

God Can Use You

> "And Saul said to David, 'You are not able to go against this Philistine to fight with him; for you are a youth, and he a man of war from his youth.'"
>
> *(1 Samuel 17:33 NKJV)*

"I can fight too." These words could often be heard on the playground during my school years. The youngest and smallest in the rough bunch didn't want to be overlooked or for others to assume that they couldn't be used for battle.

Our age and physical characteristics will never hinder us from being used by the Lord, but our mindset will. If we think we are destined for defeat, then we will stand down and be defeated. David realized that he was young in age and that the enemy had more experience, but he was confident that the Lord would use him.

What is the Lord calling you to today? You may feel that you're not ready to take on the challenge. The adversary will try to deceive you with this untruth, but the Lord was with you in the past, and He is with you right now. He wants you in His army. He is able to equip and establish you.

Empowerment Point: Everything you need is already inside you.

Prayer: Dear Heavenly Father, thank You for never giving up on me. In spite of appearances and how others may judge and criticize, I'm grateful that I can still be used by You. You alone can bring out the greatest in me. In Jesus' name I pray, amen.

Affirmation: Whether I'm young or old, my Lord has a purpose for me.

Healing Power in a Touch

"Then he said to her, 'Daughter, your faith has healed you. Go in peace.'" *(Luke 8:48 NIV)*

"*You* have tumors, and I'm sending you for a biopsy." This is what the endocrinologist stated while going over my ultrasound report. The woman of faith from Luke 8 quickly came to my mind. She had suffered for a number of years, yet she had enough faith to make it through a large crowd to touch the hem of Jesus' garment. She believed that she would be healed by touching Him. However, this story teaches us that she activated her faith to release healing.

Regardless of what's going on with your body or what the doctor's report says, press forward in faith. Believe that the same God who had the power to heal many years ago is still in the healing business. He worked it out in my favor under the microscope, and He is certainly working divine healing for you.

Empowerment Point: Facing health issues is challenging, but decide whose report you will believe: the doctor's or God's.

Prayer: Dear Heavenly Father, at times, my body doesn't feel the best. In spite of my care provider's report, my attitude of faith releases Your divine healing power. I am grateful daily for Your wonderful works of healing. In Jesus' name I pray, amen.

Affirmation: Whatever strikes against my body, I am healed in Jesus' name.

Hoping for Answers

"Trust in the LORD with all your heart,
And lean not on your own understanding."
(Proverbs 3:5 NKJV)

*U*nexpected tragedies and other occurrences happen and questions arise. Why did this thing transpire? Could something different have been done? These are just a few questions we ask when life leads us somewhere surprising.

A number of years ago, my father succumbed to injuries he sustained from a tragic work-related accident. I was at the tender age of twenty when he died, and many questions ran through my head. The answers to some still remain a mystery.

Confidence in the Lord is the most appropriate action when something inside you demands a response. His ways don't always seem logical, but they do line up with His perfect will. You may never receive some answers, but the Lord knows what to reveal and what to hide. Accept His perception, place your heart in the Lord's hands, and believe that He cares about the inquiries that concern you.

Empowerment Point: The Lord has all the answers, and He will keep you at peace in the midst of your wondering.

Prayer: Dear Heavenly Father, some events in my life have made room for confusion. Being the Creator of all things, time, and seasons, You will give me peace in the midst of it. I'm letting go and trusting You with these unclear things. In Jesus' name I pray, amen.

Affirmation: I will raise my head and trust in the Lord's answers.

In His Presence

"She had a sister called Mary, who sat at the Lord's
feet listening to what he said." *(Luke 10:39 NIV)*

Martha occupied herself with household duties in preparation
for and during Christ's visit, but Mary had an intense
yearning to be seated right at His feet and take in every word He
had to say.

Often, the most primary tasks can lead us to be worn, overwhelmed,
and distracted from what's most important: getting closer to Christ.
Taking time away from busyness and positioning ourselves to listen
to Christ speak is to be valued.

Your schedule is never too much for Christ to bear. Of course,
you must tend to everyday life affairs, but likewise be eager to sit
with the One who cares for and loves you the most. Do it just because
of who He is.

Empowerment Point: In that sacred place, clarity and more is
revealed.

Prayer: Dear Heavenly Father, it's a privilege and an honor to be
able to enter into Your mighty presence at any hour. Thank You for
always standing by to hear every matter of the heart and to provide
divine instructions. Everything that I need is in the overflow of Your
abundant love. In Jesus' name I pray, amen.

Affirmation: Because of who Christ is in my life, I long to talk with
and hear from Him.

Invisible but Still Moving

"Now faith is the substance of things hoped for, the
evidence of things not seen." *(Hebrews 11:1 NKJV)*

A few pieces of certified mail was sent from my local post office. Online tracking later indicated that one piece hadn't left the origin site. However, it reached its destination in the expected timeframe.

Just because we don't see a particular situation evolving doesn't necessarily mean that nothing is happening. God is always working. Too often, we depend on our natural eyes and emotions rather than the Spirit, which exercises our faith.

For everything that looks to be at a standstill in your life, turn your vision around and persuade yourself to see progress. Believe that God will leave no loose ends and that He is surely changing things for the better.

Empowerment Point: Trust that things are shifting at just the right speed.

Prayer: Dear Heavenly Father, as the Creator, You see and know everything. Help me to place my faith solely in You for all things. Your Word and presence assure me that You're always moving in my life. In Jesus' name I pray, amen.

Affirmation: In spite of what I see in the natural world, I believe that something greater is happening.

It's Not Your Battle

"'You will not have to fight this battle. Take up your positions; stand firm and see the deliverance the LORD will give you, Judah and Jerusalem. Do not be afraid; do not be discouraged. Go out to face them tomorrow, and the LORD will be with you.'"
(2 Chronicles 20:17 NIV)

We don't always know what's up ahead and around the corner. It's good to be prepared spiritually for the worst. Although he was in much distress when he learned what was coming up against him and his people, Jehoshaphat knew how to let go and release the conflict to the Lord. He trusted in the Lord's wisdom and instructions, and he believed victory was in His hands.

You don't have to wrestle with everything. When you're at the crossroad and you don't know what to do or which direction to take, the Spirit of the Lord is a helper. He is a refuge within which fear will disappear.

Empowerment Point: Let go and let God.

Prayer: Dear Heavenly Father, having You by my side is such a blessing. There are times when it seems I'm outnumbered and defeated. I appreciate You stepping in on time and prevailing on my behalf. In Jesus' name I pray, amen.

Affirmation: Right now, I release control to my Lord.

It's Turning Around

> "Now behold, an angel of the Lord stood by him, and
> a light shone in the prison; and he struck Peter on
> the side and raised him up, saying, 'Arise quickly!'
> And his chains fell off his hands." *(Acts 12:7 NKJV)*

Our Lord is a miracle worker, and He will suddenly do the spectacular. Peter's imprisonment didn't prevent him and others from petitioning the Lord for rightful freedom. Even while Peter was under heavy security and waiting to be executed publicly, the Lord sent an angel to reverse the adversity and loose the chains.

In some form or fashion, you've endured injustice. It's possible that you know someone who is incarcerated due to biased circumstances. Know that an angel from the Lord is assigned to the scene. Be of good cheer and expect nothing less than a positive and miraculous change. The path to freedom is quickly on the horizon.

Empowerment Point: Nothing stays the same, and help will come in peculiar ways.

Prayer: Dear Heavenly Father, what appears impossible to man isn't for You. Some things will work against me regardless of how truthful I am. It's awesome to know that You can turn it all around in the blink of an eye. In Jesus' name I pray, amen.

Affirmation: He is shifting my atmosphere.

Jealousy Never Prospers

"So when the Midianite merchants came by, his brothers pulled Joseph up out of the cistern and sold him for twenty shekels of silver to the Ishmaelites, who took him to Egypt." *(Genesis 37:28 NIV)*

Envy causes strife and separation, and it provokes catastrophic behavior. Too often, it takes root and surfaces in biological families, the workplace, church congregations, and various other areas.

In spite of his brothers' mistreatment of him, Joseph's troubles eventually worked in his favor (Genesis 41:39–41). It's evident that the spirit of jealousy and the devious acts that derive from it will not flourish. In fact, jealousy only incites the Lord to render more favor toward the victim.

Be the best you! Accept and appreciate that whatever has been predestined for you is only for you. It has your name on it. Don't miss out by aiming to gain what others possess. When you wait on the Lord to give you your own, it will be supreme.

Empowerment Point: Celebrate others and trust what the Lord has for you.

Prayer: Dear Heavenly Father, if ever the spirit of jealousy reigns in my heart, please reveal it to me. I submit my prayer for the things You have in store. While being formed in my mother's womb, all that is mine was already aligned. In Jesus' name I pray, amen.

Affirmation: I will live in contentment and rejoice for others.

Let Your Voice Be Heard

"And when he heard that it was Jesus of Nazareth, he began to cry out and say, 'Jesus, Son of David, have mercy on me!'" *(Mark 10:47 NKJV)*

We can only wonder what the outcome would have been if Bartimaeus had not called out to Jesus for help. If he had remained silent and wallowed in self-pity, it's possible that he would have been left in his present condition.

It's possible to miss an opportunity to get the Lord's attention. However, it's comforting to know that He wants us to make our requests and concerns known to Him. This doesn't mean that we have to speak or shout out loud. More importantly, we're called to express a heart of sincerity.

If you desire something from the Lord, don't let others persuade you to keep quiet. Activate your faith and rest in assurance that the Lord is willing to do it.

Empowerment Point: Whether with a loud cry or a quiet whisper, don't be afraid to let Him know what you desire.

Prayer: Dear Heavenly Father, thank You for always watching over me. You are a helper at all times, and you're ready to hear my cries. Let me not forget that my faith pleases and capture's Your attention. In Jesus' name I pray, amen.

Affirmation: The Lord will answer me.

Momma's Words of Wisdom

> "'For I know the plans I have for you,' declares the
> LORD, 'plans to prosper you and not to harm you,
> plans to give you hope and a future.'"
>
> *(Jeremiah 29:11 NIV)*

*D*uring my teenage years, I had a neighborhood friend and schoolmate who loved the street life. One afternoon while I was preparing to go out with her, my mother in so many words and with a calm demeanor warned me that my association with this friend wasn't for my good. Momma's words penetrated deeply, and I canceled my plans.

Exactly fourteen years after my mother's death, I saw this old friend from afar and barely recognized her. It was evident that her struggles from her former years were still present. I whispered up to heaven, "Thank you, Momma."

Many times, the Lord captures our attention by speaking through others, particularly those who care about our well-being. The prophet Jeremiah by way of a letter spoke to the captives in Babylon with instructions, warnings, and hope for them to gain a prosperous future.

Someone may be speaking into your life. Be alert and wise. Their words could impact and divert the direction of your life in positive ways.

Empowerment Point: Imparted words of wisdom are like fresh water quenching a strong thirst.

Prayer: Dear Heavenly Father, help me to recognize Your voice through people who are in place to assist me along a positive path. Wise words from others are truly a blessing. I'm grateful to You for showing true love through others who are concerned about my future. In Jesus' name I pray, amen.

Affirmation: I will not take life-changing words for granted.

More Than Enough

"I know how to be abased, and I know how to abound. Everywhere and in all things I have learned both to be full and to be hungry, both to abound and to suffer need." *(Philippians 4:12 NKJV)*

The desire of a man's heart is to have plenty. Some have everything they could possibly dream of and yet feel unsatisfied.

Do you recognize that the Lord is more than sufficient? The apostle Paul knew what it was like to be lacking and to have abundance. Regardless of what state he found himself in, he remained satisfied. Why? Because he understood that his fulfillment was never dependent on how much he had in the world, but on the Lord, who has everything.

You may experience one trial after another, but hold steady and know that there is still plenty to be grateful for. Be mindful not to let what may be lacking move you into a place of discontentment. The Lord is all that and He will provide what you need.

Empowerment Point: Seeking gratification solely in worldly things will lead to emptiness.

Prayer: Dear Heavenly Father, I'm so glad that You are all that I could ever ask for. When I look through the eyes of the world, it appears at times that all I seek will never come. You remind me daily of my many blessings. In Jesus' name I pray, amen.

Affirmation: All of my needs are met as I wait on the Lord.

No Big I's and Small U's

"For God does not show favoritism."
(Romans 2:11 NIV)

*U*nfortunately, many are convinced that living a lavish lifestyle matters the most, and they belittle others who have a lower status. However, God formed all creation and humanity to care for one another the same, regardless of status.

Your walk may be different from the person next door, and vice versa. You've been blessed with a particular gift, and the same is true for your colleague in the next cubicle. Therefore, no matter what position you're in, don't make anyone else feel less valuable. There is no one bigger than God. Stepping on others to get what you want is not in God's favor.

Empowerment Point: Make others feel important and appreciated.

Prayer: Dear Heavenly Father, I'm so grateful that You are in control of everything in heaven and on earth. I give You control of my entire being and my interactions with others. Help me to be mindful of the fact that no matter what I own, You've allowed it to be so. In Jesus' name I pray, amen.

Affirmation: I will honor and respect God's creation in all that I do.

No Dumping Ground

"As iron sharpens iron,
So a man sharpens the countenance of his friend."
(Proverbs 27:17 NKJV)

*S*ometime ago, I became acquainted with a Metro rider. The focus of my conversations with this individual was frequently their troubled marriage. However, it seemed no effort was being made by either partner to save the union. One day, a question came to my spirit: "How is that you're seeking God for a spouse, but you allow negativity to be poured into you?"

It's wonderful to feel comfortable in sharing with other people, especially during turbulent times, but some people intentionally use others as dumpsters. We empower one another when we converse at an optimistic level.

Decide to be an encourager during your encounters regardless of how bad one's circumstances may seem. Motivate one another to be wiser, better, more loving, and equipped for good works.

Empowerment Point: Being there for another doesn't mean you have to play God, receive anything and everything, or try to resolve all of their issues.

Prayer: Dear Heavenly Father, I want to always flow in Your love. Increase my understanding when I receive from and deposit into others. I will honor You at the center of my communications. In Jesus' name I pray, amen.

Affirmation: I will seek wisdom to reject anything that hinders me from growing stronger and empowering others.

One Judge

"There is only one Lawgiver and Judge, the one who is able to save and destroy. But you—who are you to judge your neighbor?" *(James 4:12 NIV)*

Whether some of us want to admit it or not, we have the tendency to pass judgment on others based on the color of their skin, their outer appearance, or their circumstances.

Judging others signifies arrogance and pride. This certainly doesn't get the Lord's attention. He knows the details and specifics about us all. Many people have earned law degrees and have been granted the authority to rule in courtrooms. However, at the end of this human life we live on earth, there is only one final Judge.

You can't always see everything going on behind the scenes with another person. In conversations between people, much is left out and not revealed on purpose. Exhort and leave the rest in the powerful hands of the Almighty.

Empowerment Point: If you ever find yourself judging others, stop and look at what's going on with yourself.

Prayer: Dear Heavenly Father, I give You thanks and praise for enabling me to be sensitive when encountering others. You command that we assist one another out of love and not to take Your place as judge. Expose where I've failed my brother or sister in this area. In Jesus' name I pray, amen.

Affirmation: Showing love toward others is my ultimate goal, not criticism.

Only One Who's True

"Now when all the people saw it, they fell on their faces; and they said, 'The LORD, He is God! The LORD, He is God!'" *(1 Kings 18:39 NKJV)*

Not everyone will believe, and many will heed their own false gods. There are even many counterfeits within the body of Christ.

Truth indeed prevailed on Mount Carmel. When the false prophets of Baal called out to their god, they couldn't get an answer. In fact, they got no reaction at all regardless of how loud they cried out. Yet when the prophet Elijah prayed and called on the name of the Lord, He responded with fire.

It's good to know that we don't have to sacrifice a bloody bull to prove that the Lord is real today. He reveals Himself constantly in and through mankind.

Therefore, you don't ever have to doubt or wonder who's who. Our Father in heaven is the beginning and the end.

Empowerment Point: His daily working power is more than enough to make us believe.

Prayer: Dear Heavenly Father, I give You thanks for reminding me that You're the only true One and that no one could ever take Your place. Thank You for revealing Yourself to humanity every day with Your faithfulness and many blessings. I constantly seek Your face and presence, desiring to know more about You. In Jesus' name I pray, amen.

Affirmation: I will always acknowledge the only true and living God.

Payday Is Coming

"'I will repay you for the years the locusts have eaten—
the great locust and the young locust,
the other locusts and the locust swarm—
my great army that I sent among you.'"

(Joel 2:25 NIV)

*I*ndividually and collectively we've had a great deal taken from us, invaded, and destroyed over a number of decades. In many cases, this is the Lord's way of disciplining us, aiming to get our attention and to get the best out of us as His children.

Many folks spend a huge amount of time living in defeat and concentrating on what has been wiped out. Still, we have a Father who is committed to His promises.

What's been stolen from you and your family? What is the enemy holding? Whatever it may be, the Lord has declared that you're getting it all back with an increase. He is merciful even when we are an unworthy mess. Claim what has already been confirmed and paid in full.

Empowerment Point: It's never too late to turn to the Lord and get what belongs to you.

Prayer: Dear Heavenly Father, You've shown me kindness when I'm not all that You expect me to be. You've made a way for everything that has been shattered in my life to be refurbished. I'm honored that nothing less than the best is what You desire for me. In Jesus' name I pray, amen.

Affirmation: I expect increase, overflow, and more than enough in return for all that has been seized.

Peace Right Now and Forever

> "'The glory of this latter temple shall be greater than the former,' says the LORD of hosts. 'And in this place I will give peace,' says the LORD of hosts.'"
>
> *(Haggai 2:9 NKJV)*

*T*he house of the Lord was being reconstructed for the second time, and the people were apprehensive before this prophetic word and encouragement came forth. It wouldn't just be a regular house, but a temple filled with God's assured peace and blessings.

No matter what we set out to do to exalt God, He is with us and there will be peace. Refuse to accept the negative or to be shaken by what's opposing you right now. Grab ahold of the spoken word and let the peace of God reign in every dimension of your being.

Empowerment Point: You create your own space of tranquility not based on your circumstances but based on where you direct your mind.

Prayer: Dear Heavenly Father, I'm pressing to keep my thoughts and ways wrapped in Your divine promises. It is there that Your peace surpasses all human understanding. Whatever lies ahead has Your glory stamped on it. In Jesus' name I prayer, amen.

Affirmation: My home and everything attached to me will be blessed with the peace of God now and forever.

Perfect Fit

> "For just as each of us has one body with many members, and these members do not all have the same function, so in Christ we, though many, form one body, and each member belongs to all the others."
>
> *(Romans 12:4–5 NIV)*

When you hear the words "perfect fit," they may remind you of your favorite outfit hanging in your closet. However, how do you view yourself in the body of Christ? Do you find yourself wasting time comparing yourself to others?

God has given each of us strong abilities, spiritual gifts, and talents. Spending quality time with Him directs our steps in seeking out what He has for us to accomplish. As we continue to grow and mature in Him, He will disclose our purpose.

Perhaps you're wondering where it is in the "body" that you fit. Remember that you're not strange or different, but perfect and unique in the eyes of God. He has the perfect spot for you. No one in humanity has been left out or overlooked in His creation.

Empowerment Point: There is a divine purpose for all who are in the body of Christ, and you're perfect.

Prayer: Dear Heavenly Father, everything You have assigned specifically to me before I took my first small breaths is perfect and special. I will not misuse my time by desiring another's place, but rather I seek You for my own. Just knowing that there is a place for me in Your kingdom is an awesome blessing. In Jesus' name I pray, amen.

Affirmation: He will indeed make room for my gifts.

Positive Connections

"He who walks with wise men will be wise,
But the companion of fools will be destroyed."
(Proverbs 13:20 NKJV)

People in our circles either have a positive or negative influence on our existence. Whenever we are in the presence of others, it's wise to pay close attention to our conversations and body language.

Do we miss the mark? Certainly we do. Do you gossip at the coffee station and in the breakroom with your colleagues? Before you even drive your car out of the church parking lot, are you degrading brothers and sisters? Are you the peacemaker in your family, or have you settled for a position on the drama team?

You want what pleases God to flow upon you. Therefore, make a conscious effort to be more aware of your conduct in the company of others, and be careful of who you permit to lead you.

Empowerment Point: Take the high road; refuse to stop and linger on an imprudent path.

Prayer: Dear Heavenly Father, when I'm connected to You, I'll attract those who represent the nature of Christ. Reveal to me when I'm not exercising wisdom regarding my companions. Thank You for the individuals You've placed in my life who have genuine hearts to help me grow. In Jesus' name I pray, amen.

Affirmation: I am my own person, and I take responsibility and accountability for my associations.

Power to Change and Restore

> "'I will give you a new heart and put a new spirit in you; I will remove from you your heart of stone and give you a heart of flesh.'" *(Ezekiel 36:26 NIV)*

There was depravity in the land of Israel, which provoked the Lord's consequences. A word from the Lord came promising change and restoration in the heart of man.

We can spend an enormous amount of time hoping and praying for the hearts of others to be changed, particularly our loved ones. It's important for us to understand that the power to make this happen is out of our hands.

In addition to praying for those closest to us to be changed, we also must be willing and have a yearning desire to be transformed ourselves. We are flawed individuals by nature, and we have partaken directly and indirectly in displeasing behaviors.

Is there something lingering in your heart or in the heart of someone you desire to be changed? The Lord desperately wants to do a new thing in you and those you love. He can cleanse and make any heart more like His.

Empowerment Point: Release and let the power of the Lord do what's necessary.

Prayer: Dear Heavenly Father, search my heart and remove anything within it that doesn't exemplify You. I've placed my tainted flesh before Your Spirit many times. I'm grateful to You for providing me with the opportunity to embrace change. In Jesus' name I pray, amen.

Affirmation: Day by day I'm being renewed.

P. U. S. H. (Pray Until Something Happens)

"And he stretched himself out on the child three times,
and cried out to the LORD and said, 'O LORD my
God, I pray, let this child's soul come back to him.'
Then the LORD heard the voice of Elijah; and the
soul of the child came back to him, and he revived."
(1 Kings 17:21–22 NKJV)

*M*ost of us who are mothers have experienced how significant and powerful the word *push* is in the labor and delivery room. In the final stage of the birthing process, constant pushing and hard work are necessary to bring forth a new life.

It is easy to grow weary in prayer, particularly during a period of time without any apparent progress. What would have occurred if the prophet Elijah had decided to pray once versus three times? Of course, none of us can answer this, but the prophet's powerful and fervent prayer is evidence that we must not give up on our petitions to God. Just as an expectant new mother is coached during her temporary season of pain, we must pray until something happens.

God is birthing and raising the spectacular in you. God is changing the atmosphere every time your heart reaches out in prayer. Regardless of how long you've been praying, believe that it has already happened.

Empowerment Point: Don't wait until it happens to pray; pray until you see results.

Prayer: Dear Heavenly Father, my heart is filled with prayers. When there is no hope or signs of wonder, let me know that You are there. Grateful I am, because I know it is all successful. In Jesus' name I pray, amen.

Affirmation: I feel the Savior's power all around me, and I believe that He is pushing on my behalf.

Related but No Relationship

> "'I will walk among you and be your God, and you
> will be my people.'" (*Leviticus 26:12 NIV*)

*M*any kinfolk, whether they are local or long-distance, struggle with developing and maintaining a true, meaningful connection. Some occupy the same household and share a variety of things, but still don't know one another intimately or have a solid relationship.

Just like with relatives, the vast majority of people don't have a secure, structured, and consistent bond with our Father. God yearns to have the same relationship filled with promises with mankind that He established with the Israelites. He also wants His people to live by His decrees.

From the beginning of your life, while all of your organs, blood vessels, skin, and entire image were being formed, you belonged to God. Seek your security in salvation and build a profound relationship with Him. Talk with God in prayer and yearn to hear from Him at a heart-to-heart level.

Empowerment Point: When you're close to the Creator, you'll see His hand at work in other relationships.

Prayer: Dear Heavenly Father. I don't want to just follow traditions and routines. Let my heart and entire existence earnestly be in tune with Your Spirit. In spite of my imperfections, thank You for desiring to be in true relationship with me. In Jesus' name I pray, amen.

Affirmation: I am a child of God.

Release You and Keep It Moving

"There is therefore now no condemnation to those
who are in Christ Jesus, who do not walk according
to the flesh, but according to the Spirit."
(Romans 8:1 NKJV)

The teaching in this verse is easier said than done at times, correct? Absolutely. You're probably thinking, "No one can begin to fathom what has happened in my life or what I've done."

It's important that we not only sincerely forgive others for their offenses, but that we also forgive ourselves. The magnificent thing about God is that He instantly forgives us once we seek Him, and He continues moving forward. We beat up on ourselves when He has already thrown it all in the sea of forgetfulness. We waste valuable time holding on to our transgressions mentally and physically.

You are a precious child of God. Let your issues go; stay connected to the most powerful One and He'll show you how to keep going in peace.

Empowerment Point: Refuse to permit anyone else or yourself to hold you hostage.

Prayer: Dear Heavenly Father, free my mind of any guilt, shame, and negative labels that have discouraged me and tried to define who I am. Regardless of my mistakes, nothing and no one can hinder Your forgiveness. By taking a step each day and releasing everything that holds me captive, I look forward to the future. In Jesus' name I pray, amen.

Affirmation: I am free in Christ Jesus.

Secret Keeper

"A gossip betrays a confidence,
  but a trustworthy person keeps a secret."
                                    (Proverbs 11:13 NIV)

*R*egardless of how much we love someone or the number of years we've known them, it doesn't mean they can be trusted with private information. Not everyone we encounter has our best interest at heart. One thing is assured though: we can place our confidence in God.

Sometimes silence isn't necessarily an indication of being aloof, but rather is a wise illustration of true confidentiality. Demonstrating discretion when disclosing is crucial in reaching our destiny.

Weapons seen and unseen are being formed at all times, sometimes even by those who are closest to you. Share your heart's desires and experiences cautiously and as the Master leads. Above all else, trust Him to show you a confidant.

Empowerment Point: It's common for others to give you a reason to lose confidence in them, but God never will.

Prayer: Dear Heavenly Father, You know all there is to know about me. Help me to be wise when divulging information to others. Give me an ear to hear and eyes to see who is really for me. When You declare anything over my life, no matter what the enemy tries to do, You will perform it. In Jesus' name I pray, amen.

Affirmation: My secrets are always safe with the Creator.

Secured Flight

> "'While I was with them in the world, I kept them in
> Your name. Those whom You gave Me I have kept;
> and none of them is lost except the son of perdition,
> that the Scripture might be fulfilled.'"
>
> *(John 17:12 NKJV)*

*I*n the movie Non-Stop starring Liam Neeson in the lead role, there was reason for great concern and anxiety in the air. In the midst of the threats coming in by text, the characters also discovered that a bomb was on board.

When the unforeseen is before us, it is human nature to become fearful and lose our way. Christ's disciples had great work ahead of them, and He knew it wouldn't be easy to fulfill. Therefore, He prayed that they would be guarded from all evil and corruption.

Our travel on this flight of life will present uncertainties, dangers, and fears. However, Christ is interceding before the Father on your behalf. Whether everything seems to be going well above the clouds or if you suddenly feel an uncontrollable decline at a fast rate of speed, know that you are being protected in the safety of His personal aircraft.

Empowerment Point: Seatbelts were designed for a temporary purpose, but your security in Christ Jesus is everlasting.

Prayer: Dear Heavenly Father, in the name of Jesus Christ alone is my divine protection. At times, this universe is an unpredictable and scary place that can make achievement seem impossible. Whatever my method of transportation and wherever my predestined path leads, I seek refuge in You. In Jesus' name I pray, amen.

Affirmation: Whether I go up or down, I will never be lost in the world with my secured Savior.

Self-Reflection:
Inside Beauty, No Mask

> "But the LORD said to Samuel, 'Do not consider his appearance or his height, for I have rejected him. The LORD does not look at the things people look at. People look at the outward appearance, but the LORD looks at the heart.'" *(1 Samuel 16:7 NIV)*

*S*ocial media is the hot spot for sharing photos and so much more related to external beauty and fashion. On the other hand, if we were asked to examine who we really are on the inside, could we answer truthfully about the condition of our hearts?

One day in the office some time ago, my colleague complimented my hair, saying, "You look like you're going to a wedding."

I replied, "Yes, my hairstylist does a really good job."

Yet during that time at the end of most days, tears would roll uncontrollably down my face. I had to remove the mask and face the real terrors on the inside. My outer appearance spoke one thing, but my heart and everything that was taking place in my life on the inside was speaking something different.

Samuel was warned by the Lord in considering a candidate for king not to judge based on outside appearance. The Lord looks beyond that into our hearts.

The Lord wants to work on you from the inside out and make you whole and complete. True beauty radiates from within and requires much effort. Therefore, be patient with yourself. Be quiet and investigate what's happening on the inside.

Empowerment Point: In time, your outside beauty will fade, but what reflects from inside you will speak the loudest.

Prayer: Dear Heavenly Father, if I had a million tongues and opportunities, I couldn't thank You enough for creating me in Your own image. If I replicate anything that's not pleasing to You, make me virtuous. Change me from the inside out. In Jesus' name I pray, amen.

Affirmation: I am fearfully and wonderfully made.

Stand by Your Blood

"But Ruth said:
'Entreat me not to leave you,
 Or to turn back from following after you;
 For wherever you go, I will go;
 And wherever you lodge, I will lodge;
 Your people shall be my people,
 And your God, my God.'" *(Ruth 1:16 NKJV)*

*R*uth had the opportunity to honor her mother-in-law's request and return to her native home. She refused, committing to be by Naomi's side with compassion wherever the Lord would lead.

The Lord gave us our family members to love and be there for them. This often fails; especially in times of hardship, there is much dysfunction and brokenness in our families.

Be sensitive to the needs of those in your family. You may not be in agreement with all related to you, but never let this interfere with you lending a listening ear or a shoulder to cry on. Move out of your place of comfort to walk by their side. This may require a significant sacrifice, but it is well worth taking a stand. Embrace your loved ones with everything in you.

Empowerment Point: Stand with your family in prayer and watch the Lord do the miraculous.

Prayer: Dear Heavenly Father, I appreciate the relatives You have given to me. Where we are weak in our connections and relationships, I ask You to intervene and restore. Let me be quick to respond in love with a heart of sympathy and a positive attitude. In Jesus' name I pray, amen.

Affirmation: I am my brother's and sister's keeper.

Stay Calm and Give God Your Heart

"Tremble and do not sin;
when you are on your beds,
search your hearts and be silent." *(Psalm 4:4 NIV)*

nger is a natural emotion, and it can be incited by a variety of events. However, we must not permit it to have control over us and provoke anything contrary to God's will and ways.

During his times of trouble and mainly prior to resting through the night, David encouraged himself, remaining composed and reflecting on God's Word. This indicated that he refused to lie down in distress. It was imperative that he gave his heart and any matter troubling him to God.

Wow! Many of us have fallen asleep uptight countless times only to awaken feeling worse and facing the same dilemma. Therefore, it does no good when we harbor anger. It only leads to destruction.

Has anger taken a foothold in your life? Perhaps it's not the matter at hand that has triggered it, but something you permitted to take root in your soul many years ago. Don't give iniquity an invitation. Open up your sword of the Spirit (Bible) and trust in the God of serenity, and He will refresh your heart.

Empowerment Point: Becoming infuriated wastes times, power, and energy, and it hinders your ability to love freely.

Prayer: Dear Heavenly Father, it's very easy for me to get upset and respond accordingly. I'm thankful for Your holy and divine Word, which is able to speak and calm any negative emotion. At times when I could have done the unthinkable, You kept me. In Jesus' name I pray, amen.

Affirmation: I will rest in God versus permitting negative emotions to overpower me.

Take Small Steps

> "And the LORD your God will drive out those nations before you little by little; you will be unable to destroy them at once, lest the beasts of the field become too numerous for you."
>
> *(Deuteronomy 7:22 NKJV)*

Being ambitious and eager to advance is certainly a positive spirit to have, but many tasks require taking one step at a time. Many people disregard this theory only to find themselves engulfed in circumstances that are too enormous for them to handle.

The Lord is aware of what we are able to handle. He holds the blueprints to get us just where we need to be. Sometimes He has to clear the way before we can move into a certain territory. There could be individuals and unseen mechanisms waiting to do harm. Our steps are ordered for our good.

Your challenges and the desire to grow could lead to unexpected places. Don't faint and lose heart. You can't handle everything in your own strength. Let Him direct and intervene little by little.

Empowerment Point: This world moves at a fast pace, but you can safely walk one step at a time with the Lord.

Prayer: Dear Heavenly Father, there are times when I try to take on that which is too big for me. You are in control of the victories and challenges that surface. You know exactly what and how many steps I should take in every experience in my life. In Jesus' name I pray, amen.

Affirmation: Every step I take is pushing me closer to my destiny.

Temporary Residence

"For here we do not have an enduring city, but we
are looking for the city that is to come."
(Hebrews 13:14 NIV)

No matter what we acquire here on earth, we shouldn't get
to comfortable with it. It's all temporal, and we should
take on the same attitude Christ our Savior had during His suffering.

The Hebrews received comforting words of exhortation and
warning to refrain from clinging to anything in this sinful world.
They were to be set apart and live out their faith for the sake of Christ,
and during their time on earth, they would experience persecution.

Would you like to extend your stay on earth? Some folks
probably would accept this invitation from our Father if it was
offered. Realistically, we all know that this isn't possible. You
have somewhere to go. Make preparations for that permanent stay
in heaven.

Empowerment Point: Live out each day to the fullest as though it
is your last.

Prayer: Dear Heavenly Father, I own nothing here. Whatever I
possess is all because of You. Let me not forget that I'm only passing
through this world and that my eternal home will offer far more than
this world ever could. In Jesus' name I pray, amen.

Affirmation: I believe He has gone ahead and prepared a place for me.

Temptation Overruled

"Then the devil left Him, and behold, angels came and ministered to Him." *(Matthew 4:11 NKJV)*

Temptation is inevitable. Thanks be to God that there is a wayof escape.

Christ understands man's affliction during temptation. Imagine being led into the desert. You're starving, and on top of that the devil keeps coming and running his mouth. For some, this would probably be overwhelming and too much to withstand. The Savior was challenged three times, but He rejected the adversary and stood strong by fighting with the Word of God.

Temptation doesn't have to rule you. Quickly dismiss it by speaking and standing on God's Word. It's one of the most powerful weapons you could ever use to flee.

Empowerment Point: Enticement will greet you, but words of power will provide the strength to stand undefeated.

Prayer: Dear Heavenly Father, thank You for Your understanding and willingness to suffer with me during trials. You love me enough to make a way for the temptations of the world to not devour me. I am blessed that I have You and the Word to set me free. In Jesus' name I pray, amen.

Affirmation: I have power within and spiritual weapons to resist all that comes to destroy me.

The Power of a Parent's Prayer

"'And give my son Solomon the wholehearted
devotion to keep your commands, statues and
decrees and to do everything to build the palatial
structure for which I have provided.'"

(1 Chronicles 29:19 NIV)

*S*tanding behind our children in prayer is vital. King David
prayed on behalf of his son Solomon regarding the building
of the temple. Although God had called Solomon for the task, he
was young and inexperienced. He prevailed through King David's
prayer. Later, Solomon was appointed in his father's place and
prospered as king.

Your children may be tiny tots, or they may have grown up and
met adulthood. In either case, pray fervently in strong faith that
God's will be manifested in their lives. If a challenging situation is
on their path, be the first to petition God on their behalf. Connect
with other parents in prayer. There is no greater gift you could give
your children than prayer. It releases the power of God over every
area of their lives.

Empowerment Point: Through your prayers, God is moving
mountains and empowering dreams in your children's lives.

Prayer: Dear Heavenly Father, my children are precious gifts from
You. Whatever stage they are in or wherever they are, make me
aware if I've faltered in prayer for their well-being. Thank You for
hearing my many cries and requests for my children. In Jesus' name
I pray, amen.

Affirmation: I will keep my children in prayer without ceasing.

The Power of Words

"In the beginning was the Word, and the Word was
with God, and the Word was God." *(John 1:1 NKJV)*

After returning home from a lunch date with one of my
spiritual mothers, I began to explore the wonderful
unexpected gifts I had received. One in particular was a devotional,
*Moments of Peace in the Presence of God: Morning and Evening
Edition.* A few days later, one of the devotions, "Surrender All,"
contained powerful and penetrating words. I was reminded that
laying it all down at the Lord's feet and allowing Him to handle the
details of my life was all that was required.

Since the beginning of time and God's creation, words have been
significant. The most influential words one can receive is from the
Word of God. Our words share wisdom and knowledge with others,
and His Word does the same for humanity. In times of darkness, it
is the brightest light.

Pay close attention to words. They may be big or small, but they
have a meaningful purpose. Your greatest blessing may be wrapped
up in them.

Empowerment Point: Words have the ability to not only change
perspectives but lives.

Prayer: Dear Heavenly Father, Your Word is my guide and protection.
The peace, comfort, and wisdom it provides is always refreshing. It's
gratifying to know that Your Word is in order and consistently on
time. In Jesus' name I pray, amen.

Affirmation: I am tremendously blessed when my words are
acceptable in His sight.

The Unexpected Turns for the Good

> "But Naaman went away angry and said, 'I thought
> that he would surely come out to me and stand and
> call on the name of the LORD his God, wave his
> hand over the spot and cure me of my leprosy.'"
>
> *(2 Kings 5:11 NIV)*

*W*hether it's divine healing for ourselves, healing for someone dear to us, or another expectancy, disappointments are likely to occur in life. Naaman assumed that the Lord was going to heal him in one way, but He chose to cure in a different manner. Only after submitting to the prophet's request did Naaman find out that it all turned out for his benefit, and healing was bestowed upon him.

Even when you can't trace Him, the Lord is performing wonders. His ways may be contrary to what you're anticipating, but have confidence in Him. Our bodies and everything else belongs to Him. Therefore, He knows exactly how to accomplish what needs to be done.

Empowerment Point: When things appear to be going in the opposite direction of what you want, bless the Lord anyway.

Prayer: Dear Heavenly Father, it's simple to assume that having things go my way is most beneficial. Thank You for loving me enough to show up with detours and new instructions. It's humbling to know that a new avenue can work for my good. In Jesus' name I pray, amen.

Affirmation: I will stand strong in the Lord.

Trap of Deception

> "And it came to pass, when she pestered him daily with her words and pressed him, so that his soul was vexed to death, that he told her all his heart, and said to her, 'No razor has ever come upon my head, for I have been a Nazirite to God from my mother's womb. If I am shaven, then my strength will leave me, and I shall become weak, and be like any other man.'" *(Judges 16:16–17 NKJV)*

Deception by any means is the enemy's charge. Our souls are always at stake, and if we are not cautious, it won't be difficult for us to fall prey to schemes.

Samson's story probably reminds many of us of trickeries that have crossed our paths. Some come with warnings, and others come by surprise. We must search every spirit through the eyes of God, not our natural eyes. Samson was unable to detect Delilah's treachery and true nature because of his love for her. As a result, he surrendered and suffered grave consequences.

Perhaps the snares are already in position for you, but keep looking up. Don't take the fall. You're an overcomer.

Empowerment Point: Protect what has been placed inside you.

Prayer: Dear Heavenly Father, everything assigned to my life is precious in Your sight. Obstacles and distractions seem to always be present. Nevertheless, I know that Your power is working within to cover me. In Jesus' name I pray, amen.

Affirmation: I claim freedom from every spirit that intends to destroy me and my purpose.

Under Fire in the Workplace

"In your relationships with one another, have the same mindset as Christ Jesus." *(Philippians 2:5 NIV)*

The majority of people in the workforce spend long hours at their place of employment. With a variety of personalities working close together, unfair circumstances, misunderstandings, and conflicts are to be expected.

It's been declared in so many words that whatever happens to us shouldn't be our primary focus; rather, how we respond to and manage situations is what's most important. Sometimes giving no response or action moves God, ushering in favor. Our attitude should reflect God. We see this example of Christ displayed while the apostle Paul was encouraging the church of Philippi.

Not everyone in your work environment knows Christ. Meditate on the apostle's approach whenever you feel like the heat is on. When your mind is in the right place and united in agreement with Christ, nothing ignited by the spirit of darkness can burn or destroy you.

Empowerment Point: Fire burns physically and emotionally, causing grave harm, but it is not more powerful than the mind of Christ.

Prayer: Dear Heavenly Father, help me to exchange my carnal and negative mindset for the mind of Christ Jesus. I am grateful for the job and career You've entrusted to me. Every day before I enter my workplace, cover me in Your armor. In Jesus' name I pray, amen.

Affirmation: My mind belongs to Christ Jesus.

Walking Away

> "All things are lawful for me, but not all things are helpful; all things are lawful for me, but not all things edify." *(1 Corinthians 10:23 NKJV)*

*I*t's not always an easy thing to do, but sometimes it's necessary to turn from certain things and even some people who are not beneficial for our well-being. We have the freedom to make choices that may look and even feel good, but they can be detrimental.

The church of Corinth was encouraged that their freedom didn't give them the right to participate in whatever they desired. It's still true that whatever we engage in should bring the Lord glory. Not everyone can go where the Lord is taking you. We not only help ourselves to move forward, but others as well when we act according to what glorifies the Lord.

You've been given the power and authority to walk away from that which is not pleasing in the eyes of the Lord. Whenever you're uncertain about anything, walk closer to the One who holds nothing but what's upright for you.

Empowerment Point: Choose what's right and release without regret what's blocking your walk.

Prayer: Dear Heavenly Father, I trust that You alone know what's best for me. Help me to move beyond and turn completely away from things and people meant for destruction. Let my choices always exalt You. In Jesus' name I pray, amen.

Affirmation: I must make detours in my life and walk completely away from some things.

While You Were Out

"This is the message we have heard from him and declare to you: God is light; in him there is no darkness at all." *(1 John 1:5 NIV)*

Whenever I look at the words "While You Were Out" as they stand in big, bold print on a message pad on my desk, the entire pad takes on a whole new meaning and purpose. Along with these particular words, it contains a variety of blank spaces for pertinent details, but the most significant to me are the blank box in the upper right-hand corner titled "Urgent" and the section titled "Message."

We have all have been "out" in a number of ways and areas, not just physically, but by walking in the dark in life. But there's good news! There is an "Urgent Message" from the Lord: While you were out, He telephoned to let you know that you're not forgotten. While you were out, He stopped by to put His arms around you. While you were out, He answered your prayer calls and He desperately wants you to call on Him again. While you were out, He wanted you to know that He's coming back again soon.

Empowerment Point: Not every message is appropriate and filled with light, but the Lord's are always worth receiving.

Prayer: Dear Heavenly Father, I give You thanks for coming to my rescue when I was down for the count. There are no words more powerful than Your own, and I can depend on a promising message from You. I will continue to bless You at all times for sending the right message in the appointed season. In Jesus' name I pray, amen.

Affirmation: The Messenger will come see about me.

You're on Somebody's Mind

> "In the first year of his reign, I, Daniel, understood by the books the number of the years specified by the word of the LORD through Jeremiah the prophet, that He would accomplish seventy years in the desolations of Jerusalem. Then I set my face toward the Lord God to make request by prayer and supplications, with fasting, sackcloth, and ashes."
>
> *(Daniel 9:2–3 NKJV)*

*H*ave you ever been in desperate prayer and wondered whether anyone else would be concerned? The Lord who reigns from the powerful spiritual realm is faithful and full of mercy and empathy. Without us being aware of it, He will position us in the hearts and minds of others.

Daniel interceded on behalf of his own people regarding their captivity. He offered a heartfelt prayer from the soul with much sacrifice.

Believe that the Lord is touching the right people to intercede for you. They are ringing and shaking the heavenly domain. You're not in this thing alone.

Empowerment Point: You're not forsaken, and He is hearing your intercessors.

Prayer: Dear Heavenly Father, in my weakest state, I appreciate others who are moved even in the wee hours to cry out for me. You alone know the mind and heart of every man. Thank You for receiving petitions that knock on the gates of heaven, carrying my name. In Jesus' name I pray, amen.

Affirmation: I am spiritually connected to others.

Your Presence

> "For this reason I have sent to you Timothy, my son whom I love, who is faithful in the Lord. He will remind you of my way of life in Christ Jesus, which agrees with what I teach everywhere in every church." *(1 Corinthians 4:17 NIV)*

A dear friend of over three decades and I attended a memorial service in support of another friend. The embraces, tears, and exchange of words told us just how much our showing up really meant to our friend.

Timothy was sent as an example for other believers to follow. He was faithful and one whom God trusted to represent His character and to encourage the people of God. Just by our presence, our faith can comfort, strengthen, heal, and speak volumes to others, regardless of what state or situation they are in.

Let God lead you whenever you find yourself wrestling with questions like, "Should I attend? Should I stay home? What do I say?" Although feelings of having nothing to give or offer can creep in, you just may be the one He has chosen to be an example or to bring a contagious hug and smile to bless another. Perfection is never required; just be you. Your presence does matter, and it will make a difference.

Empowerment Point: The moment you walk into a room and any other vicinity, you release energy that affects others, whether it's positive or negative.

Prayer: Dear Heavenly Father, let me be someone who portrays Your shining light. Bless me to be in the midst of others with an unselfish and compassion-filled heart. Thank You for the reminder that my attendance can impact the lives of others. In Jesus' name I pray, amen.

Affirmation: I will strive to be an atmosphere changer.

Your Work Is Not in Vain

"For God is not unjust to forget your work and labor
of love which you have shown toward His name,
in that you have ministered to the saints, and do
minister." *(Hebrews 6:10 NKJV)*

Many people feel as though their work is useless. They
assume that no one is paying attention, and they question
whether their efforts are making a difference.

God is to be revered first in all of our callings and duties. His
unconditional love is exemplified to the utmost when we work hard
and pour something into ourselves, others, and the universe.

Believe what you hear from God, and don't accept being placed
in a position with a title just because man desires you to be there.
Never convince yourself that your work is worthless or too small.
God is always watching, and rest assured that He will not forget. You
won't always receive a pat on the back or reward from others, and
you may have more against you than with you, but there is a prize
to claim in glory.

Empowerment Point: Keep doing what you do best with the love
of Christ Jesus in your heart at all times.

Prayer: Dear Heavenly Father, everything I am called to do is
because of You. Let love consistently flow from my heart whenever
I aim to do anything. Above all else, let my work bring You glory. In
Jesus' name I pray, amen.

Affirmation: My work for His glory will never be overlooked.

*"Whatever God has called you to do, it may not be for **everybody**, but
it's for **somebody**." —Prophetess Juanita Bynum*

A Blessed Invitation

*Y*ou now have an opportunity to receive and secure your salvation by accepting the Lord Jesus Christ into your heart as your personal Lord and Savior. You're not required to be perfect; none of us ever will be. You don't have to wait until your circumstances and struggles are resolved. He desires to welcome you right where you are at this very moment.

Speak His Word out loud from your heart:

> "That if you confess with your mouth the Lord Jesus and believe in your heart that God has raised Him from the dead, you will be saved. For with the heart one believes unto righteousness, and with the mouth confession is made unto salvation."
>
> *(Romans 10:9–10 (NKJV)*

Now seal your salvation with prayer:

Dear Heavenly Father,

I come to You in the name of Your Son, Jesus Christ. I admit that I am a sinner and that I need Your forgiveness.

I believe that Jesus Christ shed His precious blood and died on the cross for my sins. I am now willing to repent and turn away from my sin.

I confess Jesus Christ as Lord of my soul, and with my heart I believe that You raised Jesus Christ from the dead. I accept Jesus Christ as my personal Lord and Savior, and according to Your holy Word, right now I am saved.

Thank You Father, for forgiving me and making me Your child. I commit my life to following and living by the teachings of Jesus Christ. In Jesus' name I pray, amen.

Congratulations, and welcome to God's family! Step out in faith. Seek Him and ask to be led to a church that teaches and preaches based on the Word of the only true and living God. This is an important decision that you'll never regret.

Peace, blessings, and much love on your new journey.

Commentaries

Praise for *Blessings to Inspire*

"*T*he compassion found in the pages of *Blessings to Inspire* is life changing, a convicting life application that keeps you turning the pages and wanting more. Jacqueline uses her powerful testimonies in a remarkable way to touch, encourage, and challenge all who read this book. Each devotion lifts your spirit with living words of Scripture, integrating practical life experiences we encounter in our daily lives. God's Word and her journey connect in a dynamic way to capture and equip you with inspirational spiritual tools, insights, and affirming words that will empower you to use *Blessings to Inspire*. This is a must-read for anyone wanting to take their relationship with God to the next level."

—Yvette Davis

"*Blessings to Inspire* is indeed the product of a true spiritual and anointed warrior. This powerful Spirit-filled book imparts hope and encouragement. It will touch and impact your life. I highly recommend this book for the saved and unsaved."

—Corlos Morris

About the Author

"For many are called, but few are chosen."
(Matthew 22:14 NIV)

Jacqueline Denise Stinson is a native of Washington, DC, an inspirational writer, editor, poet, and author. She is the proud mom of one adult son, who is the star in her life. On her mother's side, she is the fifth child out of six, and she is the oldest out of two on her father's side. She is truly grateful to the Lord for the son He entrusted her to raise, all four of her older sisters, and one baby brother.

She discovered her passion for expressing herself through written words in her personal journals and diaries as a young child. After losing her mother to lung cancer in 2002, Jacqueline rededicated her life to the Lord, and her outlook on life changed significantly. Writing was like medicine for coping with the grieving process, and it helped her win her battle with depression. She started writing poetic expressions, and she produced her first poetry book, which was published in 2009. In 2013, the Lord released her to write inspirational devotions. She started publishing and encouraging many through her personal e-mail chain and now on social media. It became evident over the years and through many confirmations as she began to walk closer with the Lord that her writing is a magnificent gift and blessing in her life to inspire herself and many others. Jacqueline is a member of the Temple of Praise, Washington, DC, under the awesome and life-changing leadership of Bishop Glen A. Staples and Pastor Walter L. Staples.

Since 2014, she has faithfully served as a volunteer with the Christian Pen Pals Ministry (CPP) based out of Hickory, North Carolina, where she encourages and shares her gifts with many across the United States who are incarcerated. She also contributes as a writer and editor to CPP's newsletter.

She truly believes that we constantly need a word filled with life, truth, and power, and that the Word of God is faithful in reminding us that we overcome by the word of our testimony (Revelation 12:11). As she continues to venture on this journey for the Lord's glory, her sincere prayer is that all who cross this path will see less of her but more of Christ Jesus, and can declare for themselves without a shadow of doubt, "I have been chosen."

Contact the Author
(Comments and reviews about this book are welcome)

E-mail: blessings2inspirepoetrycafe@gmail.com
msjaedee@comcast.net
Inspirational Word Website: www.blessings2inspire.com
Facebook: Jackie D. Stinson
Instagram: godinspiredwriter4life

CPSIA information can be obtained
at www.ICGtesting.com
Printed in the USA
FFOW02n2207211217
44192875-43629FF

9 781545 619346